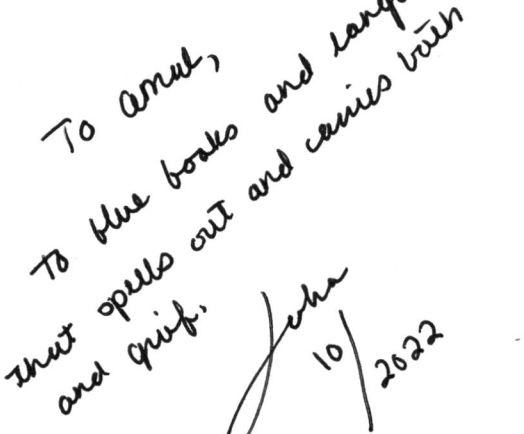

To Amul,

To blue books and language
that spells out and carries both love
and grief.

John
10/2022

WALT MCDONALD FIRST-BOOK PRIZE WINNER

Rachel Mennies, *editor*

your blue
and the quiet
lament

poems

L U B N A   S A F I

TEXAS TECH UNIVERSITY PRESS

This book is typeset in Crimson Pro. The paper used in this book meets the minimum requirements of ANSI/NISO Z39.48-1992 (R1997). ♾

Designed by Hannah Gaskamp
Cover design by Hannah Gaskamp

Library of Congress Cataloging-in-Publication Data

Names: Safi, Lubna, author. Title: Your Blue and the Quiet Lament: Poems / Lubna Safi. Description: Lubbock, Texas: Texas Tech University Press, [2022] | Series: Walt McDonald first-book prize in poetry series | Summary: "Poems chronicling stages of grief after a cousin's murder at the hands of the Syrian state"—Provided by publisher.
Identifiers: LCCN 2022002773 | ISBN 978-1-68283-139-7 (cloth)
Subjects: LCSH: Grief—Poetry. | LCGFT: Poetry.
Classification: LCC PS3619.A3555 Y68 2022 | DDC 811/.6—dc23/eng/20220121
LC record available at https://lccn.loc.gov/2022002773

Printed in the United States of America
22 23 24 25 26 27 28 29 30/ 9 8 7 6 5 4 3 2 1

Texas Tech University Press
Box 41037
Lubbock, Texas 79409-1037 USA
800.832.4042
ttup@ttu.edu
www.ttupress.org

For Hisham

From the beginning it belonged to distance as the blue color of the mountain does.

—W. S. Merwin, *Heartland*

The winter air splinters
your blue, and the quiet lament
of some cool spring
cuts through your groves.

—Federico García Lorca, *Elegy: To Silence*

Contents

III.

IV.

V.

CONTENTS

Foreword

In Lubna Safi's lush, devastating *Your Blue and the Quiet Lament*, blue builds a field for grief and its testimonies, on which its speakers bear witness to state violence, illness, and the iterative traumas of living in diaspora. This field—fragrant with winding jasmine, sour lemon pith, hand-harvested earthy saffron—summons the collection's landscapes into both the body and mind at once: we move, sometimes within the space of a single poem, among Syria, America, Spain, and elsewhere.

The speakers of *Your Blue and the Quiet Lament* travel on Safi's lyric waves between grief and joy, the particular and the vast, as when one says to her lover in the poem "Human longing found trapped in amber" only a couple of lines apart: "I tell you about the scab of my cousin's death. . . . In the dark that draws and loosens the bodies of lovers, we try." Safi insists we see the whole blue field in each poem and, by extension, in her speaker's testimonies: she shows us how trauma undercuts pleasure, how pleasure transforms grief, and how these powerful forces work together to construct an understanding of home. "Maybe there exists," she writes in the poem "Archive of a diminishing return," "a timeless wisdom that survives failed economies, wars, maybe / even its own definition."

Throughout the collection, Safi transforms the blue field, which holds (here, in the poem "Blue variations") the color "of blues notes, of edges, of memories of your eyes, of piercing, of the afterimages of Lorca's words, of stones and storms . . . blue tent of refugee camps, of veins." It marks mourning and fills golden vistas, real and rendered alike, with watery grief. The author's mother, who once coated her hands with "clarified blue smudges / of an azure sky," one day stops painting with blue altogether, and Safi—in "My mother no longer paints with the color blue," an early poem in the collection—introduces powerfully the reach of her grief, interfering even with her creation:

> I cannot explain what happened,
> only that it emerged out of the blue.
> The painter, she used scorched earth to capture
> the stain of what had passed beyond the window.

Later, we witness the mother in the hospital in the poem "Jasmine," where her "samples of defeated blood / seeped through and colored / the blue flowers purple." Grief leaves the canvas and enters the body; the blue field washes with the body's work. Safi's speaker sees not just the "exposed parts" of her mother's body, though—here the jasmines vine, "climbing" from the "shadow on her chest." The sterile room of suffering fills still with a tender, delicate sweetness.

While some figures in *Your Blue and the Quiet Lament* struggle with illness, the speaker's cousin dies violently under the specter of state violence. The poem "Ta'ziya" testifies to this directly, showing us the cousin's brutalized body:

The sigh-with-no-relief chimes of at-least-we-have-a-body to bury,
to wash, to run wet hands on the wounds like clay.

Before the camphor-cleaned torture marks and lotus-infused bullet holes,
we mined the cold-metal flesh of shrapnel missed by the autopsy.

Cousin, with whose touch is your skin crawling beneath the shroud?

Cousin studs the collection with sharpened grief—a blue blade. "[O]ur love," says the poem's speaker, "the noise that ancient warriors made before battle." The speaker and her family mourn him separately and together across poems. His loss, and his lost body, become one of *Your Blue and the Quiet Lament*'s vital omnipresences. The interplay of epistolary conversations with, interruptions from, and appeals to the Spanish poet Federico García Lorca—from whose poem "Elegy: To Silence" the collection's title comes— form another, as in the poem "Shot and buried with Lorca":

I used to hear the dead speak like verses
in Lorca's poems, barely audible . . .

they appeared to walk right out of the words,
poor creatures in a dream groping for God.

We behold both Lorca the man and Lorca the creator in *Your Blue and the Quiet Lament*. Through him and his work, Safi summons the speaker's own grieving process into the collection, shaping our understanding of the relationship between artmaking and personhood.

Your Blue and the Quiet Lament is the first Walt McDonald First-Book Prize in Poetry winner whose entire acquisition process—from my first encountering Safi's incredible poems in mid-2020 to writing down these words on a December 2021 afternoon—took place under the pandemic's heavy winding sheet. I note this both for the extraordinary fact of it, to testify to the importance of the making of books in such a time, and to witness how that weight imprinted my experience with her work. This foreword focuses on grief, only one of this collection's many taut and vital threads, because grief is the blue field on which I began to read Safi's work, and the one where I still do. It is perhaps where you, the reader, begin to read today as well. I join you in this ritual—ritual, whose "hands," writes Safi, "reach into the graves / of words"— to lift grief's shroud and, if we cannot lift it, to attest to its weight together.

It is my deep honor to share and celebrate Lubna Safi's dazzling book with you, the prize's twenty-eighth winner, in this difficult year—now more than ever, as we say so much these days. It is a book that I learned from, and one I have needed.

RACHEL MENNIES

your blue
and the quiet
lament

I.

Although

It was Friday—no—weeks ago someone said.
Where had they taken him?
What does his mother know?
Had anyone, in the last hour, held the blue reins of his eyes?
No one had known he was gone,
and when they learned it had already begun.
No one insisted they knew why it happened.
The only witnesses were already dead, and the water
reluctant in its role couldn't be blamed for taking the space of air.
Petrified color of torture, the floors grayish
in a prison just outside the faded edge of the city.

My mother no longer paints with the color blue

My mother sees nothing with her hands
canvassed across her lap except the shade
of every blue she ever painted. Her other paint
tubes clotted red, purple and black.

When she paints, my mother looks without
seeing me. Her fingers feathered
with the clarified blue
smudges of a sky,

fortified blues of the ocean, the melancholic
sapphires of the late-night hours,
not white for snow, just bluish marks
of what passes, or blue nothing at all.

I cannot explain what happened,
only that it emerged out of the blue.
The painter, she used scorched earth to capture
the stain of what had passed beyond the window.

Shot and buried with Lorca

I used to hear the dead speak like verses
in Lorca's poems, barely audible,
Ay ay ay
      Ay ay ay
            Ay ay ay ay
their jawline punctured by putrid air,
flesh oozing from the mouth
of a page full-bodied
they appeared to walk right out of the words,
poor creatures in a dream groping for God.

Not Lorca after the cantilevered prayer
Not August with the daylight fading
Not the curve of a rifle hit the head
Not his face washed thin by the last sunlight
Not a tree where the body fell.
Instead, a November fog, and the eleventh day over
with a choking sound. I skip lines to avoid the end
of the poem but I can't outrun the news that has
reached me, that his mother withheld,
that his father didn't know. That my cousin had
covered himself with God and died in a shroud.

Photograph with jido in Damascus

His palm open, fingers curled
to catch the landing of my small fist—
egg-tight in the clutch of a nest.

Though he shed most of it around the cap,
my grandfather's hair never turned white.
The Syrian saying goes: he got out of it
like a wisp of hair in dough.
But this poem is not about Syria yet.

My mother had kneeled down
because in this still life we are at eye level.
Behind her, the porcelain plates, and beyond,
just before the flash, jido still holding my fist—
what we could not bear to see, even then.

Every morning I walk

A crow lands twitching its tail. Another bird trying to catch up to a fervent flock. The others hover in the air as if vibrating into blue parodies of the sky.

I meet the same people at different moments and places. Never once do I say
hello. My morning walk, a throat-clearing.

The disemboweled gourd left half-entombed in the bushes so it can decay almost out of sight.

Between two working men moving a tree fallen from the wind:

—I wasn't told what would happen, and no one else was either.—I'm going to back up the truck now.

The rake protests the asphalt, its sound enough to grind the grief to a halt.

I walk right after a night that has drenched everything—leaves, plastic bags, discarded toys—
in place.

Water accumulated to a drop on the tips of branches, birds gathered on one side
of the phone line. All around me the danger of imbalance.

To say something of the truth

You say: I trembled like thunder.
        But your body is not a cloud.

You say: I passed by the sharp fragrance of a hidden flower.
        Fire can be drawn even from the greenest wood.

You say: the eyes are windows to the soul.
        In your saying, I notice your eyes disappear.

        I, too, live where no domes or minarets silhouette the horizon,
        though I still wake up before the sun outlines the orange sky

        between the eclipses of two swallows,
        because the heart itself is a matter of curves.

You say: I can't write *lover* without *over*.
        The word *deserted* also implies an *oasis*.

You write: The soul resembles fire.
        No, the soul is more concealed than that.

You say: saffron is more valuable than opium,
you have to harvest the flower by hand.

        An eyelash has fallen onto the surface of your face.
I pinch the thinning skin and ask you what to do with it.

Protasis with lemons

If my mother hunched in the kitchen with a heap of lemons that she peels with a blunt knife.

If my mother with the lemon she eats in slices like someone else's orange.

If my mother, squeezed and strained, and the lemon juice dripped down her arm, leaving sticky flesh-colored trails.

If my mother even in the Syrian summer that swelters, refuses ice in her drinks.

If my mother, damp to the touch and coarse like lemon peel.

If my mother's jaundiced country.

If my mother, who puts little sugar in her lemonade because it reacts with the medication, stirs the pulp drink into small cups.

If my mother laughs, the sour pucker a sign of something she won't say.

If my mother with a determination like a seed in the deep flesh of a lemon.

Deep song

Poeta revolucionario García Lorca
called the cante jondo, the unspoiled cry
of life. Or just the death-drive
said poeta non-grata Freud.
Or the pulse that cannot be flesh,
I said when I realized that Granada was
a cemetery—the whole city,
its public parks and pedestrian crossings.

Bleary-eyed, I had followed a life-art turn
to Parque Lorca when, nearly to my destination, I ran
into a man at the edge of the sidewalk.
His cane like a finger pointed and drew me in.
A Spanish fulano with a maudlin mandolin expression
plunged down from the unforgiving border of a path
I had side-stepped. Not wide enough for the spiraling
of a poet's generous language, like a throat
just before it contracts, in my ear.

Portrait of a mummy in Granada

She leans across the table in a small café in Granada,
her hair limp against her shoulders,
the angular outline of her arms, her hands
crossed over one another on her lap,
to tell me I remind her of a mummy.

In an image of an image I am refigured
to a relative twice-dead removed,
a mummy almost too small to be a woman,
too tight and wrapped in herself.

I did not ask her to clarify the portrait
of the painted woman of fayyum,
or what she meant when she said
"You have her nose from this angle."

She might have meant it the way my grandmother means
when she tells me to face a mirror
and discard those reflections
that don't suit me. The difficulty of fixing myself
in frames like an object suspended
and gilded, pulling a face from its features.

My hand reached out of habit for the fruit
across her at a table as ancient as the city.
The difference a layer makes
when it wraps and covers and resembles.
The way it must have looked when I unraveled
the fabric framed around my face,
like seeing a grape for the first time without its skin,
an eye held between two fingers,
unadorned in my mouth as I chewed.

Blue variations

Blue is the blue of distance, "the ink that I use is the blue blood of the swan" (Cocteau), of the sea, of the faraway, a discriminating blue, of your eyes, of memory, the blue of baby boys, of glaciers, of a last light, the great blue chord of a nocturnal symphony, of being cold, of shallow holes, of tender bruises, the gathered blue of my mother's laughter, of once in a moon, of mountains, of blueprints, of the hottest fire, of silence, of nostalgia, of herons, of dreams, lakes, and skies, of reading *The Holy Book*, the blue-black of my grandfather's hair and Hayden's cold mornings, of the horizon, blue taste of summer, off-blue of concentric waves, of elsewhere, "this blue that opened the way to you" (Bennis), of feeling, of late nights, of blues notes, of edges, of memories of your eyes, of piercing, of the afterimages of Lorca's words, of stones and storms, blue like thought, like time, the past and present blended together, blue tent of refugee camps, of veins, faded blue of childhood's tongue, of cold lips, glacial blue of the Arctic nights, of God's unfolding hand (C. D. Wright), of our pale dot, of the tepid pool water, of the elemental hue of the upper sky "that seems to retire from us" (Goethe), of the typical heavenly color (Kandinsky), blue turning deeper and deeper before going out.

Still life in the morning

This early, the vapor dances
like a dervish over the teacup.

Sugar crystallizes
disobeying the water,

deep and deepening still.
A thought to stir it, to start

the rush, the ripple.
My finger beside the spoon,

bent sickly, unfeeling spine.
Between two shoulders my soul

fits staid and unseen.
I've not known how to leave

places gracefully. Your hand glides over
mine, until your fingers push off. Only then

do my eyes open. The rush, the rippling over
yet the essential thing untouched.

In two parts my love

Plastic from mystic sleep, pliant night beneath pillowy sky,
I was asleep when they rushed you headfirst to the emergency room.

You awoke to a morning drenched in wires and that hospital smell.
The monitor that guarded your heart all night, caught your wavering breath.

All night, while I slept, the one-sided touch of a needle on your veins. Of latex
against your skin. X-rays of bones and what doesn't want to be known. And still

the inconclusive results. They couldn't strip you down far enough to see what God could.
Our God the all-knowing, you had said, and I turned the corner to my childhood.

That night, a mourning sound and I fell with the hint of a memory. A cooing dove
is a sign of loss in the Arabic lyric. I wanted to be devastated by something,

but for what? These words? So much work to cast off grief. My whole body heaving
against the tip of me. My face in two parts, my love in divided languages.

I only saw your truncated slippers in the line of light waiting for you to retrace your steps.
My eyes waking at their unencumbered pace. My ignorance cannot be bullied by the light.

In another universe my father leaves with his knife

Somewhere in Damascus, cement against bone,
　　　　my father broke his wrist in a fight.
Rotated it right out of cuff, a grind-ache that halted
　　　　future injuries, usually sustained by the handful.

Jido had taken the khanjar, the brazen crescent handle
　　　　his son had clung to, wrist-grip as if an extension of himself.
The knife that once before, my grandfather had also clenched
　　　　to teach his son the consequences choices create.
When through the pigeons my father had been raising on the roof,
　　　　went the curved khanjar's blade,
before my father packed it along with the rest of what he took
　　　　to leave Syria. The fragile joint of the body
that once articulated and moved freely.

From a distance, the country now appears like a gun,
　　　　sides with cut-off angles and uneven distribution.
My father rewrote his letters in exile, agonized over the words
　　　　etched as if by the ridge of a rib. To learn what to leave means
when in a new country he opened the suitcase to find that his knife was not there.

A grieving poem with six engravings

I settle on this color did nothing for me your absence is entombment there I remained standing when you were released laying down your last rite the linger of fog-voiced repentance.

What did I have to do with anything that happened to you the accusation creeping like a vine I recognized on the side of my childhood home the words like a mouth I thought I had forgotten.

Blue I found in the clipped feather of a bird shed and still with the moving flight in it and you had watched the clouds remembering clouds in another place feeling less alone.

You told me you were not afraid in a dream the shade is the wrong blue I woke up so it could continue inside an afternoon more final than an amputated limb.

Lorca offers me the curdled cry of a lament that leaks black from the sides of my mouth ready with self-pity in the midst of all this death says wait for the last words from the other side.

Where do you live but the where tortured by its ambiguity sawed off in the dark of revision and left only that other question the love I am sorry I did not live with you should have.

My mother falls into grief

She, standing in the doorway
weeping, outside the trees
and streets crammed, is listening
to the laughter of those who
have survived the day. This
morning she had answered
the phone. Told to wait, again,
over the static decades of delive-
red grief. In that time, the eye,
tongue, and hand disobey.
Then, the cut of voices.
Did they [...] his body [...]?
She says, *God [...] them.*
And says, *[...] down their houses,*
then says, *over their [...].*
Let the [...] in their heart
that has [...] the country
[...]to their graves.
And finally says, *[...] God.*

II.

Ta'ziya

A day like any other, then, to stomach the intrusion of condolences.
       Certain intrusions into the heart are acceptable, like slicing
              into a marine animal to find that it has three.

The sigh-with-no-relief chimes of at-least-we-have-a-body to bury,
       to wash, to run wet hands on the wounds like clay.

Before the camphor-cleaned torture marks and lotus-infused bullet holes,
       we mined the cold-metal flesh of shrapnel missed by the autopsy.

Cousin, with whose touch is your skin crawling beneath the shroud?

No *then*. We did what the remaining know to do—*through*. We scraped
a song from the throat,
           kin kin kin kin cousin kin kin kin kin
cousin cousin kin kin cousin cousin
              our love the noise that ancient warriors made before battle.

The wrist-hung, the slap, the skin-punch of something so heavy
that it could be held by something as small as a day.

Human longing found trapped in amber

That night, the hum of your human body.
The long road had emerged between us.

A hollow inside me, bow-string taut and tuned to the quiver.
Like a stray remark at the edge of a long-winded conversation.

I try to escape my history, a permanent nitpicking-of-the-wound.
The scar of a homeland that won't fade.

I tell you about the scab of my cousin's death.
You are busy, fine-souled and neck-baring, unreachable even by the longest sentence.

In the dark that draws and loosens the bodies of lovers, we try.
To be gentle, *gentler* even than lovers, our eyes closed like fists, listening.

How love frauds the tongue loose when my ear catches your truant voice.
I like the rarified air around your words cut with fermented exhales.

Even the serpentine walls of your embrace.
Your heart—and this is why it's heavy—is cast in gold.

So, I don't ask you for comfort.
I've seen how your words seek what they long for and instead find the void.

On seeing the prophet in a dream

In the dream a hand reached out,
a sun-disc illuminated
a purple paradise, honey
condensed on trees.
A face clarified itself from the haze.

When I wake, its contents draining.
First shape, then skin,
then glow. In the dream he was shadowless,
and still the curved edges
of my eyes darkened
holding the imageless whole
sown and harvested by gut-feeling.

In the dream, a menagerie, a monkey, and behind it
something holy lingered,
blue and breathy,
like the outline of a body-shaped soul.
I wake up confused by the wild
and sacred.

I let in (the revelation),
the ache of a parenthetical verse.
The other gods with one syllable names
no God but two
syllabled.

My mother's evenings
soaked in the sweet sink
of holiness and still, for her, nothing.
Not even a glimpse,
no receding face or vague shape.
A name would be enough. This is how holy he is to her.

I uncover my dream, but she says nothing
is stained heart's-blood crimson with such symbolism.
My uneasy mind keeps warm wrapped up in images,
seduced by what are signs of nothing but themselves.

An explanation interrupted by Lorca

I don't remember how. I shattered my elbow during a thunderstorm
and the next morning in the sugary light, a gap gathered blue in my memory.

> *(Soul,*
Turn orange-colored.
Soul,
Turn the color of love)

I remember no skies or sunsets from my grounded childhood. I carried the dead
crow to my parents' bed after the downpour. I learned to cradle what was gone in my arms

> *I'm coming back*
> *For my wings.*
O let me come back!

before I learned to hold it in my words. I try to forget the dream in which losing teeth means
the death of a loved one. The thought falling out at the end when I heard my mother tell
him that he needed to pour water over his father. What would that assuage?

> *A marvelous coolness took hold of my body, as if to bind me with the last strands of the*
sunset's hair, & a broad avenue of light ran through my heart.

A vine can dig its roots and leaves into the walls to destroy entire foundations.
The way an exposure to what has been can enter and shatter a poet's heart.

Archive of a diminishing return

Maybe the rivers in my mother's country aren't drying up,
or maybe no one misses centuries of submerged pain, water

under the bridge. Maybe if my father had left with his knife,
he would have come back sooner maybe

soaked and old-sensed. Maybe the *shabiha* would have stayed
ghostly in their white Mercedes not pulling girls

into their rapacious mouths, their families
exchanging a hollow *maybe-they-will-bring-them-back.*

Maybe the metaphysics of writing does not need a praxis
to imagine that all this tightening is *Enough,*

enough, enough! Maybe if it were instead
them that's got shall lose, and *them that's not shall get.*

Maybe to avoid the scale of time encysted in her, my mother prays
for death, sits with the whole of history like a stone in her hands.

Maybe the diminishment of genuine embracing suggests
that it infuriates lovers. Maybe it wasn't the imprecise borders

between Iraq and Syria that dissected neighbor
from neighbor. Maybe to cut these fibers causes a sense

of dislocation, not to speak of the pain. Maybe there exists
a timeless wisdom that survives failed economies, wars, maybe

even its own definition. Maybe instead of the sky, my soul goes off
on excursions into bodies of water whose surfaces I fear are crime scenes.

Maybe the gray-sick wanting is there. Maybe even now
just outside the border. Maybe I am already up to my elbows in its foam.

A taxonomy of wind

(ending in a breath by Lorca)

When you tossed the kites, I felt the trade winds in my mouth
reliable like an ignited match. I'll call it *ruh, hawa*. At times

when the *shamal* arrives from the North—despite wonder, grief,
a Beaufort 12 desire—I am unable to move. *Saba,* not enough air

to extinguish a flame. I'll call it the-clouds-bellowing-above-you-like-petals.
Nafas, to call you in Arabic, I say, *my breath*.

Let me call it my-mind-ran-unfocused-to-its-exhaustion.
Khamaseen, summum, the gales that shut you in and rage

beyond the window like a taunt. To say a thing is windswept
breathless or blown. To call it ruined-from-taking-too-long.

Smoke-streaked sky and I couldn't stop swaying my hips,
an ancient movement to bring about a different kind of weather.

When, in a moment of passion, the heft of a mirage, you said *please*
and I called it *like a bird that collides with the wind, your kiss on my lips.*

Atlal

1.

When ancient poets stood over their lover's campsite ruins,
and in the aftermath of an intimate detonation, kindled odes—
their beloved riven between the beams of the past and a fallen wall—
they discovered in the ashes the logic of unchanging grief.

2.

Armed forces move in and out of view as meandering shadows.
Lorca said once that he wished he could be like his forebears, the defeated
Arabs. He was shot beside a tree that bent over him
like a gravedigger over a hasty burial.

3.

My mother agonizes over the living membrane of a charred earth,
longs for Spring's furious waters and for the elegies of the old poets.
I ask her about places empty of people,
her voice, toward an answer, is soft like ash and a passing thought.

An essay on witnessing

And when your Lord brought forth from the children of Adam, from their backs, their descendants, and made them bear witness against their own souls: Am I not your Lord? They said: balā (yes), we bear witness.

—The Holy Quran (7:172)

In this poem, I will explore the glottal separating balā (like coda)
from balā' (like coma, or like the second syllable of forget).

A glottal is the expansion of the throat. Then, the crisis of a prostrating tongue.
In middle America, I prayed by turning each cheek ocean-ward.

From my mother I inherited God, her blue-hued love, a dominant trait
to pass judgement, and an otherwise good certainty. On days when talking

quickened our hearts and our fears clarified the stakes, yes, I felt her grief as if
she were saying, I only have this name. In this poem, I will explode, body to the bone,

my mouth misting, it begins to sound like one syllable *light light light*. Cries
clenched behind writing teeth, dawn breaking as I broke, I prayed by turning

against my own soul. My eyes possessed whatever my sight fell upon.
Balā' so I strengthened my jaw by chewing on mountains. I followed river

currents to realign my spine, truncated the flow of words from my throat.
My body grew, but the look of one who would one day die never changed.

Prayer beads

Between her hands
the intervals are
perfect thirds. Thumb-sized

tongue-tripping prayers on a thread.
Sandalwood praise sanded down
by eager fingers.

A chastening rhythm
moves my mother, her
entire body a cross-legged hinge

forward and back as she mouths
God's glory. Her hands perform
a nail-biting ritual

with longing tucked under
her tongue. About God
everything is necessary.

She says to me: *Each time
I speak to God, you interfere.*
Then says, this is the last time,

but she's fingered the beads
thirty-three times for the third time.
In the economy of her breath,

each little bead, the entire truth.
One of my mother's rote ways
of provoking feeling.

From behind, my mother's back
is like a hill, a holy body,
a feeling as fact.

Her breath joins the air,
and the echoes keep her up
at night. *Yes, I bear.*

If God fills her, then
give her strength. It is my weakness
not to remember this.

Mother grief

Her Adamic son reaching in the dream
for the fruit, its rotten taste seared
on the tip of her tongue when she wakes up.
To wash it out, she summons the water's pantheon
from a darkened eyelid—the descent
into a mother's over-ripe grief.
Maybe he hadn't endured a dry cough
that didn't subside until he was
beneath the water. And maybe she had stood
up when they came for him, stood in the way
unmoving like the footprint of an animal
in the snow or like drawings of waves
etched on sand-stone graves
(chastened blue surrender).
They took the sight right out of her eyes.
She suffered profound visions of the water,
her son's head in its unblent currents,
ears ringing with Arabic words of love that scorch his tongue
on their fire-blue taste only to say
what would give his mother grief.

III.

Poppy

Since the August sky fled
with the pressed flowers of its evening dusk.
Since the Barada river retreated
and its current smoothed the riverbeds to their final inches.
Since the street signs in familiar letters were replaced
by slant counterparts in a rigid alphabet.
Ever since the quiet
receded in a scatter of afternoons, one after the other
after the other. Since that phone call,
and eleven years of ruptured silence
grieving while fingering her prayers beads. Since
my mother left the hemmed borders
of a thousand-elegized city
she can no longer return to. Since marriage
since three children, since little conversation,
since the early hours of a long war. Ever since
she catches her body over the bed,
careful not to tear the surgical incisions,
blood as red as her made-up lips
when she wore her wedding dress
at the first departure, the old silver
around her chest, and a feeling near her throat.

Jasmine

The first time I saw her spine
through the hospital gown
slit, samples of defeated blood
seeped through and colored
the blue flowers purple.
The bare IV vines spiraled
over her open mouth. No unassuming
white blossoms came alive
at night. She had tried to cover her
exposed parts with the flimsy
gown gathered around her thighs.
The first time I saw my mother's body
touched by frailty, I didn't
cry. From the shadow on her chest,
I saw the jasmines climbing.
The heart of growth fed upwards
by an entranced love pining for that place
where the flowers had first touched her.

Tuberose season

The perfumer in Damascus fills crystal bottles full of flower
wound. He says the tuberose has a short season. He measures
out travel-size containers cleared to leave Syria. The smell
wafts from the bottle as he dips it towards her wrist. She rubs
together skin and tuberose and oil. How does the smell reach
her fingertips, her hair? The corner of her eyes—tuberose-
shaped smells. But the flowers elsewhere quickly wilt.
Whenever she walks past a flower stand. Outside of Syria
they have a weak smell, she says, so she handles them tenderly.
The bottle of tuberose, IV-drip to its last milliliter.

Gardenia

I watch as my mother recovers from beneath the hospital pillow
her prayer beads, their amber-red glints against the sterile walls.
She can move barely, but her lips are ravenous.

In tamed waters, the cream ivory petals floating.
I gave her a flower known for tenderness.
Where did she leave it? Outside, the door left open
so that the last air might slip out, and the dawn might spill in.

I heard her wake up before the light had a chance to clarify her.
I heard the soft crash of glass on the balcony.

Narcissus

A dull night, the pain intensifying,
she got up and walked to the door.
It might have been otherwise.
Years of driving past hospitals
with names of saints and men,
none brought to mind the one
who could save her. It might have
been otherwise. That night she wandered
to the edge of a lifelong question,
the explanation another way to describe
a wound. Years ago, when she turned over
her bottom lip and saw the dark redness
of her mouth, usually hidden, she didn't know
what color it should be. The cracked blue
glass misted with her laughter.
It began this way, the obsession
with the boundary between
the seen and the kept away.
Had it spread it might have been
weeks, months, a life otherwise.
Even now, her eyes seem lighter,
because of the blinding breadth
of what they are about to see.

A poet's operation

He'd like to sit with his back straight,
but Damascus is restless in his spine.
I am nine years old, and we are writing
a poem together. The words reach the end
of a line and fall off. My father
takes the words right out of his mouth, sounds
them against one another.
I am standing beside him, barely reaching his upright
shoulders, while he reasons with his choices,
the creaking aches of what holds up—
legs, bridges, spines, hopes.
The words rattle out of breath
when he decides the heart
land is laced with disease,
the metaphor a proxy for what isn't.
My father can't admit that language is a thing
already infected. The analogy unable to destabilize
anyone. A heart exposed in the language operation
emerges bloodied and muscled from its enclosed space—
the family home. At the end
the letters have become indecipherable.

How to describe being held

It was almost not you, but the circumstances held.
Of an *arrest*, which means the power of one body
over another. To hold against another will, to apprehend
between finger and thumb, to *bear* the space of a trigger
that took your life. If two people hold each other in a fight
for life, they *cling*. And to hold out of fear is to clutch.
To cup, when to hold or cradle in the curve of a hand.
To *grab* with fists, *grasp* with mind, *grip* with heart.
To *hug* is to hold close to the chest. Let me hold closer your body.
Imprisoned is to be held in the confinement of man. *Interred*
to be held by the earth. *Fasten*, is to pass from one button to another
then the entire shirt ripped off. To *keep* is to hold without release,
"keep me in your thoughts." A child *latches* on to his mother, that is,
holds her with resolute fingers. Figuratively,
to *maintain* is to hold—a whole plane of principles meant to be upheld.
Like the *nails* that to hold you up had gone through your body.
The sharp *O* of the apostrophe that addresses and holds in its enclosure
my thoughts of you. When my evenings are divine, I am held rapt in *prayer*.
My body *quarantined* an entire year—held apart—to keep the air from petrifying.
I *restrain* myself from crying out, that is hold my breath, for less time than you held yours
under water. Even when you were overcome by the *stranglehold* and your breath
gave out. *Tighten* if your fingers hold something until the untimely extinction
of air. The decision *upheld* by the court hand that labelled you potentially subversive.
In the end, your body not being held at all. Underground, the earth turns around you,
the soil moves humbly and you, like water that takes the shape of whatever holds it.
Or like a *verse*, the earliest vessel for holding consciousness. I hold your memory
in the palm of my tired hands. I tried to *wrap* you in a shroud, to hold you in one
image, but each time you scatter across the swath of my mind, a memory
in *exile*, which is to hold home in your line of sight and *yearn*, which is to be held
like a hostage by longing, by this *zajal*, a poem cooing like a dove.

They looked like they were drowning from the inside

The headline reads
like a fleshy pivot in a poem about Syrians
dying from sarin attacks.

The drowning campaign

For Idlib

The roof drenched and still chemical,
color drained from the iris
to hear it sizzling the word *sarin*.

The heat settled in bone memory,
and to face it then just newly arrived
with the capillary wound.

The rubber raft salt-salvaged
and waiting for release, bobs in the water.
The air already out like a light.

Sketch for a quiet lament

1 On the tip of my tongue, I lost you. I scoured my fingers until I was finally clean of the cone of their transparent shape. Of an acidic smell and flimsy expectations. Only to learn that they made you up with wrought words.

2 I imagine your flesh-flung body surrounded by dark water. The clear scene of your bruised face. The blood as red as a common poppy. In the cell of the secret police that took you. All eyes see through the gut.

3 Which of God's words lasted on your busted lips? Your shirt streaked like a Rorschach. They laid it out for you. The cigarette burns. The electricity. The goring of your body at the eleventh hour. Eyelids sinking. Blue with gathered promise. So close now to the heart of the color.

4 I remember you behind the rose bush. The surgical cut of thorns. The red as red as blood. I only saw the haunted flowers that you couldn't un-stem and something else. I don't have the language for it yet.

Arrival

You are grieving
and for days now
I have been
on the verge of you
carrying another hurt
an entire self-pain
fought off by your antibodies.
When was the last time
I felt you in this way?
Not a body, but ever
present like God.
When did you come back to me?
Like faith, like solid, like leaning
all at once.

For Vicenta Lorca after her son's death

Beneath the tree at the disgraced mouth of the Vega,
the earth, a borderline on the other side of which is death.

A soul has come back to the body,
as if there could be after the loss.

Mother of,
To consult the water, you need only lower a finger.
To have said this is all over when it had just begun
Out of breath and swift, like a decision or a guillotine.

Sometimes it is death with the light leaving the valley
Sometimes it is late with the blue wound loosening.

If there is no grave it's because where he was shot
is a slipstream of language reducing the world to just this world.

When they dug, the turning soil beating as if vesseled,
there was no blood, just roots.

I have a mother like this too

Mid-thought, the words running out, I say to her
while she sits with outstretched hands at the threshold of prayer
and the love drying out, I believe that more than love, it takes ventilation.
      Because it is easier than saying *our, our.*

The sayings in Arabic that tessellate the mother:
      A monkey is a gazelle in the eye of his mother,
      Drop the jar on its mouth, the daughter will come out like her mother.
      The prophet said: Your mother, then your mother, then your mother.

My mother never said to me, *you are beautiful,*
      only said the words someone else said.
I write to her, *I am tired,* in an Arabic broken by numbers
      my grief spelled out:
            I can't keep parading in front of men
a witness of what pale skin can do for desire.
      She tells me to laugh to expose the ridicule, the ritual is
just a rite of passage. For a moment, we both desire disobedience.

I've seen how she nestles the longing in her hands,
         for the sake of a city she cannot name. *There, there.*
      Without tears, how can you be sure the grief is there?

This side of prayer

I am on my knees. My eyes hold the vision
of a visible light churning the dust.

Like fire made in the space of oxygen,
my prayers are lifted by the airs of hope.

The cinder and ashes, a drama of extinction.
Breathtaking—but I've refused the word after you

in a cell your bound hands, hung by ropes made into wrists,
your body a mountain undulating in the direction of a seized country.

Forced down by an abrupt disbelief, my head burrows into the dirt.
I gather it into my palms, then try to exhale the pain and an ancient taste

of blackberries. I want you to be saved, but the pen has dried up
until doomsday. *O God*, you are this handful of dust.

IV.

The other side of prayer

I draw a line between me
and the crisis. Call it a prayer,
a threshold that can't be crossed.
Put pressure on the Lord who receives it.
Call it the line between good and evil.
Between what is and what could be
otherwise. I toe the line.
Sketch instead another one to encircle me.
Then accept that there is nothing
behind this poem's language
to shape my grief, to yield it to meaning.
Death, even when it's over, keeps me
hacking against the wolf-gray dawn.

Before he was arrested, Lorca said:
Let's pray in front of the image,
then nothing will happen.

Ghazal of the love that will not be seen

Another humpback whale washes ashore just so as to hear
the waves, half-bellied up, its body fetal. Just so as to hear?

My mother notices I keep sticking my fingers where they don't belong.
Where? Near edges, near blades, I repeat just so, as to hear

her sigh when I lay on my bed awake, shimmering sound of grief
evoking grief. I hymn the same "I'm sorry, I just—" so as to hear.

Drench, drop-feeling, the pain falling to the plane of a whisper
I close my eyes, sort blue dreams like clean socks, not just so as to hear.

Lorca, your body, broken into kindling, little fragments that caught
fire in the poems you burned, bones for the vela bell, *solamente por oír*.

Through

Rot, thick earth swollen with decay and limp
                                bodies
                                drowned
by an overworked tide metaphor, its ebb and flow
                                taken
                                wildly
to get away. A safe place besides heaven is the most
                                sought-after
                                place,
a most human fear knotted into the raft, feverish
                                feeling
                                God is.
Belly-floating on the gray sick of a quarrelsome sea
                                grief
                                drifting
through the thoughtful, the scant, the sighing day.
                                No way
                                back
from another blood-drenched morning. Eternity
                                hulled skin
                                and eyelids.
Rib-clutched, arriving elsewhere and still rubbing elbows
                                with all
                                this dying.

By the spine of the heart

My mother's voice sinks like a voice offering consolation,
the timbre of a prayer near its end, the curve
of an anchored spine. So many other things descend
in that way.

Do you remember, my mother asks, whenever the light
hit the nape of your neck, the reflection
like sunlight on gold? She has sent me back to my childhood,
to a body through which my mother's anxieties linger.

I smile elbow to elbow, crinkle like the edge of a wink
just to remember her yellow ivory flesh,
its smell of lemons and distress.
Remembering demands a supine heart
to yield to what can't be there,
like fire that isn't present in the heart
of the one who knows it.

My mother fails to understand why
moving in straight lines is a challenge
to the muscles of the heart. I'd like to tell her that
when I felt a lover's sharp prayer beads against my back,
each vertebra fingered and warped, I remembered her
hunched over, a limber descent, anchored in God.

Damascus epitaph

The graves have no names. There are no bodies to set in the dirt. Just the earth, a maddening dusk, immortal words, and dead-air echoes perfect for contemplation. A shadow moved in a ripple as if agitated in water. The sunset gave the landscape antlers of a raging deer. Jasmines balked along an infinite pavement lined with sighs and a string of sobs. A gash on the cheek, and the heart came out on its own. Here, all that could be admitted: a deserted land beneath a jagged blue cloud in the shape of a shoe.

The Quiet Lament

1

        To answer, we think about what we want from the Spring: Luck.
I waited to hear from you. Like an old believer, I was forced to become a judge. I asked this
of myself.

        I know you've come to fix the drenched roofs. Blue dreaming of
an empty sky or of drab-brown earth.

  Where to? Aleppo or Homs or Damascus or Hama or Idlib.
        Places from which a threat will be launched. Against a decay that
is invasive to the heart.
                              Are all of them, now? Extinct, that is.

2

A night of rooftops and the dry eyes of pigeons. I want to see what I see.
In front of us, we counted the number of boats that were transporting them to the sea.
                                A line of frantic length.
        In the past, in the meantime, in general, it means time is trilling.
      I want to raise a bird in the city of Karbala.   Good luck.
           You depend on your strength and your country is weak.

  I am unable to express myself. To speak of you in the silhouette of stone.
I am happy. I am angry. I was uttered by someone.
  We discussed the return while we waited for the most important   thing to do.
                            Leave.
        Even if you keep the panes bolted, I am always open.
I am always open to the canvas, especially the blue.

3

                         At the crossway, you struck out, exhausted.
We won't be able to sleep tonight.
  You are searching for a story, the knowledge of a word, but you can't write your speech in
this city.
             Jerusalem, Beirut, Baghdad, a temporary transfer.
              If we leave, we won't return.
In deception, there is no reason, no witness, no evidence of foul play.
        Shiver, take heart   in two screaming lungs.
            Who am I without you? How do I evacuate?
As for the boats, they were never resilient.

4

No angel, no angel, no one. But no one to see.

5

No, no, no, no, no.
        I insist on these words.

The reason to stay is because we have nothing to do with it. And the third reason, a secret.

A herd of ambulances form a genuine human calamity, even counting the most common incidence.

They carry causes that are weightless in the air.   Unevident sound effect
of a glorified scale that was never equal.

6
We loved the crackling blue, the peel of the sky just before the deceitful sun of both horizons.
And the country fallen asleep to prayers.
We accepted the burden of peace. To sleep without a price in the darkness, our backs to the city in a different direction.
We tasted the bitter of our titanium spit.
Steel blue of a single spoon or knife edge imprinted forever on heart and flesh and bone.

The blue that has no future, blue of an abandoned painting, blue where the wind falls short. Calamity moving in the blue of your eyes.

7
The blind happiness of your approach: bad timing and an evasive truth.
A long time, a long time ago, a long journey, a tragedy.
I want to say something wrong and ignore it.
I want to leave.
I remained in the shade you opened.
In the dark, you began to hum and the song tangled itself
with the air.

8
If I let you go, you will be killed. You say you are not afraid.
I am back in my body depleted under the failure of being human.
We suffer an attack by someone you trusted. I tell him you have grown cold.
No, the jasmine isn't our flower, and we haven't made it into a symbol for anything.
A shallow will arrives in Gaziantep, Berlin, Lesbos, Copenhagen.
I am upset with my people.   They've thrown in the air against us.
We have no choice but to occupy, and we don't have the right to occupy the country.
You prayed for this.   It wasn't good for you.

9
We prayed, too, for the sins of those who wanted to kill us for miserable wages.
The angel just barely overheard.
The human being, the first brigade of death.   Earth-bound.
Unsuccessful.
Anything is a hangover because of the pain. And the occupation of a country.
By turning away from our mourning, a mother has perished, and her love was lost.
I am tired of my people. I am tired and out of my heart.

It's necessary to make this clear and for everyone to talk about why.
   I want to talk about it. I want to talk about it. I want to talk about it.
We are praised for our weaknesses and for our values.
      We are angry, full of lamentations, we had committed our lives.

11

In the early stages of life, a person will fear every poison.
   By their good deeds they cause a drought and by them they prevent one.
You are always anxious and in a hurry.
I want to protect you from the city. There is place in the city where you give it your body.
   Suddenly, I am in the middle of the country.
      I want to be free from its compulsion.   And the roof falling.

12

As if The Family were obedient to the laws.

                                                            Ah, please.
We run.   The only option is not to be forgotten, so please read with care.
                 Ahhhhhhhhhhhhhhh Lahhhhhhhhhhhhhhh
I will go. I will leave my mind. I will not leave Syria.
               I will stay, I will live here, I will live with it.
                     An indisputable and indefinite hope.

13

   Our people, separated by days, were sent back to the city.
Lost, they were put to death.
It's possible that it won't happen. It's possible that it'll be used to scare us.
            A lazy attack, an exacerbation, an erosion of a world.
         We were forced to enter the battlefield, to occupy, to enter the city, to be taken
away.
                     After all, you will be asked about it, you said. I am sorry for that.
Our love is stuck in the side, a thorn.   In the throats, we are sure of it.
                                 No, I will not leave.
I ask you and I swear. I swear you will be tired. It will kill you.   Please hear me.

14

Damascus, but people are gone.

15

         You're shivering and exhausted, and there's no indignity in your exhaustion.
No time for people to hesitate, for different kinds of words, for other options.
               We have no good options.

16

My mother is the one who holds the secret of my honor.
         So my life is a cause that harms her.
We revel in what we are sharing with each other, and you are satisfied that you are alive.
      A delicate hand resolves our discomfort. Shivering in a fair manner.
The city of Aleppo present in the middle of a fast, fleshed out movement.
Please forgive me.   You haven't learned or you haven't shared in it yet.
      The disappearance of a country.

Please forgive me.   You haven't learned or you haven't shared in it yet.
          The disappearance of a country.

17
The city has grown in full bloom by a beautiful spring.
          From your heart your heart grows.   I want to ask for the moment
to meet us.
An airy, voluminous, volatile atmosphere.   This is a nice place
to fall off.
                    Until the well is filled, it will leave a hole.
It is unfortunate that I love the appearance and the possibility.
                                        Above, all.

18
     Meanwhile, yes, meanwhile.
We're devoted to people who live in harm's way.
                                   Leave him and let him go.
Growth, prosperity, movement.   Beautiful sounds with dire meanings.
Do not say the silence, the smile, the torment of the body, the people who bear you, as well
as the rest of the world are restrained.
If you don't walk away, you won't let us know how reliable you are.
                    A roof like a raft, an effective way to move in and out of
          the water.

19
I am not writing in your direction to furnish my dreams with violence.
I have brought you along to show you the soil, close to the only crooked tree in the open
country.
Where blood flowed and the angels looked for it.
                              To read this is not enough.
          Please tread with your utmost respect.

20
All this in the shade of Allah, and an abandoned roof.
                    After the love of language, love is not the same.
You pursue your work, your battles, your days.   Everyone will ask this of you.
          They will say loss but are free not to bear its burden.   Who could see and not
remember you.

          I am not asking, this is what I want. To make a barren picture in order to fill the blue
hours.

                    It is a matter of ventilation.

V.

Prayer in four prostrations

1

THE NAMES OF THE FALLEN ARE RECITED,
the line of protestors like teeth chattering.
A trail of smoke left by trigger-happy fingers
becomes blood congealed around the disobedient.
Hands at chest, fears at heart, they prostrate by fire.

2

With hands unfurled and thoughts tucked under arms,
THERE IS NO WAY TO GET THE KILLING TO END.
You may have gone by another hand. I tried to stop you
       by a plea that I know
like the inside of my palm.

3

I put my hands over my eyes and my lies under my feet. I can cover
any defeat with a blind spot. I know this is temporary.
       Not the matter of your disappearance. KEEP THE LIGHT ON.
I wish I had your ability, gone now, to stand up in the face of loss.

4

       We will bury the locks of your hair,
curled after the final shower. We will steep your scalp
until your wet body pulls lotus and camphor,
       as if it were created for that purpose. Then, like a symbol of the first
death, PAIN HEALS FOR GOD, we will bury you in the direction of your next awakening.

Last letter from the young poet

Inside a cell in Granada.
Lorca faced an empty paper.
Flat as a depleted heart.
In his hands an acute nakedness.
Stretched to resemble writing.
Just as he begins.
A stranger arrives.
Who has never seen him.
Painted or written or in love.
Just resigned and afraid.
With a hand he forces.
The Poet's last message.
Dear father please give.
The bearer of this letter.
A donation of 1000 *pesetas*.
For the Armed Forces. Love. Federico.

An august ending

I learned how to love from my mother,
García Lorca, and the archive of the sky
where the crescent fans out—
a sliver of a new moon in the hands of the old.

On the same day, almost nine decades later,
I was born on an earth Lorca disappeared into.
I sobbed in my room for the Andalusian
martyr. My walls were full of water
hallowed in the pipes. I crowded my poems

with a public grief. The offbeat of a sob
behind closed doors escaped like nervous laughter.
As far away as the other side of an entire country
I could hear the withered sound of an arid lament.

What did I know of sacrifice? I learned it was wax
on my mother's hands when she twisted my arm
to wring out my leftover soul. She removed
nothing, my heart was fine. I wasn't even sad.
I had just reached the end of something.

The hatred become narrower

I see you above doorways that must prop you up, your eyes the color of a diseased planet.
Despotic lines wrinkle you. There isn't a single speck of saliva in my body that hasn't
protested, screamed from the prong of my tongue. The hot air rose from where I
stood and mingled with the rest of it. Each mouth its own revolution. My teeth
gripped the places I reached for. My entire body alight. I, with a suddenly
unmuted mouth hungry as a mirror with nothing to reflect, fumble
through images left by a loss of scale, four decades since the myths
about the previous periods began. If a person survived all of this—
quiet burden, washed-out poetry, and a general Syrian pain
that looks at the corners and undersides of life—
they will still be haunted by an anger
that moves even the faintest
believers.

What my mother noticed when she didn't know it would be the last time she left

The highest mountain in Damascus makes a mess
at its feet—rocks, mosques, a tangle of trees and homes
spiral toward the square her childhood home overlooks.

Descending the summer-cool stairs then through the always
propped gates, the air and the dust play, and the light,
still leaving the building, draws a shadow

beneath the long archways of jasmine vining
around black iron grates. Unbearable at midday,
she wouldn't have stopped to look. As she leaves,

she doesn't think about the long pauses to come,
each step she takes closer to the distance between her
and her language. She has learned to leave its fire. Everywhere

else her life will change. Not in the house of the building that shades her.
What she remembers: at sunset the white petals between the iron
and leaves, the heart gone, and that girlhood smell.

A poem that ends in the footnotes

He will be younger than me

                                        alive, and older in years

dead.[1]

---

[1] A cousin never ends.

The absolute last whisper into the vatic void

The first time I heard, I didn't.
The second time, I cried.

I am beside myself. The wind drowns
and blows my cries for you,

for Lorca, for all the disappeared
and for the thin cornea of my eyes that caught no one.

Your face in my hands isn't right.
I know I can't use you like this forever.

Your blue days. I'm writing you from there.
Ritual-quiet hands reach into the graves

of words believing I'll finally hold
you in my trembling arms.

Variations on a theme by Lorca

It's likely the moon. To that glossed elegy all eyes are open. You wanted a clearer night, melancholy cries that woke the stars, and no secrets. Your mother's look falls apart in your reflection. Your soul is a changing prism, skin like a small crystal. But you don't live like you're made of glass. The breath doesn't fade from you.

Not transparent, still your verses shatter. When I read your moon poem it ruined me. I don't know how it didn't ruin the world.

You wanted the secret of spring, to know why the river runs slow and what floats above it, creaking of the just abandoned. Your Andalusian eyes thirsty for a spot where light intersects the dark, so your shadow consults the water.

No one makes you, but it is love that you intend. You've given it your word. Your body shadowed blue by the cold hand of an archangel.

The door of the cell closing and the arpeggio of your fingers, a veiled reckoning, but nothing happens.

The final reach, capsized orb floating by an altar of grates, and a hand to halt the moon's departure.

For love, in these final hours, to mean the stability of a life that was limping. To intend, as in to seize a thing with your entire hand.

Heartland

(Maybe it was because you hadn't mastered lying)

An ex-poet lover told me not to write the abstract into my poems.
Do without "East" or "West," be more concrete. Then said
he could sometimes hear my native un-English tongue. That I mangled
its expressions, misunderstood its words. Even though I grew
up speaking what eclipsed my mother
tongue. He told me not to write poems that spelled out my anguish.
Then brought me flowers on the anniversary of my cousin's death.
An obvious metaphor. It was a matter of taste, he said, of knowing how
to spice par-boiled words for the reader to savor. In a writing workshop,
a story about my mother who lived for twenty years in these United States and never learned
to speak its language. It's hard to believe, was the refrain of the story's critique.
I've translated her into my story speaking it.
My words absolved one another so that there was no harmony between us.

The gist of it

Maybe because it was God, I woke up with a crick in my neck.
I had laid down lopsided in the direction of paradise.

I've written poems because men moved me first. And now I worry
that I cling to God like a happy-meal crown.

I used to read poetry in the tenor of prayer. I followed memories
in heavy-handed circles, the way a thumb guides a knife when peeling an apple.

Now, upon first glance, things seem other than what they are. A line on the wall
that wasn't a shadow but a trail of black ants. A speck of dirt on my jacket,

and to have almost flicked off a promising caterpillar. I broke my fingers on branches
that wanted to be stems. An intimate quarrel turned into laughter at a distance.

It may be that blue is an overused color, and there are too many stones in poems
and too many Gods, and that everyone's mothers run between the lines.

Maybe a lament is just a dying expression that can still be beaconed by an outstretched foot.
I, too, placed my sorrow in the mouth of language. It was the main thing that gave me grief.

Acknowledgments

First, all thanks be to God.

This book exists because of the support and generosity of so many people. My sincere thanks to Travis Snyder and the team at Texas Tech University Press. Thank you to Rachel Mennies, for your words and for believing in this work. For their feedback on earlier drafts, thank you to Gabeba Baderoon, Rachel Richardson, and my writing group.

I thank the following publications for giving these poems their first home: "Portrait of the mummy in Granada" in *The Journal*; "Gardenia," "Jasmine," "Poppy," "Narcissus," and "Tuberose season" in *Jaffat el-Aqlam*; "Arrival" in the anthology *We Call to the Eye & the Night*; "Atlal" in *TAB: A Journal of Poetry and Poetics*; and "An august ending" in *Mizna*.

To the martyrs of Syria and to my cousin Hisham—I've buried you in these pages knowing that you are not truly dead but alive and well provided in His presence.

To my friends who held me in their kindness.

To my parents Louay and Razan for your courage and encouragement. To Rahaf, for your sisterhood and the joy of growing together. To Munir and Mackeen, for the laughter and companionship. To Mona and Kareem, for the warm surprise of sudden affection. I love you all.

To my family in Syria and across the globe, I look forward to meeting you again in a safe Damascus.

And to you, with steadfast love, because you are my tribe.

Notes

My mother no longer paints with the color blue: The lines "with this bit of clarified blue smudges of an azure sky, fortified blues of the ocean, and melancholic sapphires of the midnight hours" are inspired by Carol Mavor's descriptions in *Black and Blue*. The last stanza borrows some language from Anne Carson's *Plainwater: Essays and Poetry*.

Blue variations: This form is indebted to a paragraph from Mavor's *Black and Blue* from which it borrows the Cocteau quote.

An explanation interrupted by Lorca: The stanzas cited are from "Love, ditty of first desire," "The Return," and "Meditations and Allegories of Water."

Archive of a diminishing return: The term *shabiha* refers to a branch of the Syrian security apparatus. They were named after the white Mercedes car dubbed the "ghost" that they drove in the '70s. The lines "them that's not shall get and them that's got shall lose" are an inversion of lyrics by Billie Holiday.

An essay on witnessing: The line "dawn breaking as I broke" is adapted from Walcott's "dawn breaking as I woke."

Prayer beads: Borrows its structure from Agha Shahid Ali's "Prayer Rug." It comprises tercets in eleven stanzas to replicate the number of beads in an Islamic rosary.

Narcissus: Borrows its refrain from "Otherwise" by Jane Kenyon.

How to describe being held: The line "the earliest vessel for holding consciousness" is Jane Hirshfield's.

In *For Vicenta Lorca after her son's death*, the line "reducing the world to just this world" is borrowed from Jorie Graham.

Ghazal of the love that will not be seen: Takes its title and refrain from a poem of the same name by Federico García Lorca in *Diván del tamarit*.

Prayer in four prostrations: Capitalization is inspired by Jorie Graham's "Omaha" in *Overlord*.

Last letter from the young poet: The last lines of this poem are translated verbatim from the letter Lorca was forced to write before he was assassinated.

An august ending: The last stanza's language is indebted to Marguerite Duras.

The gist of it: The last line in this poem is adapted from Lisel Mueller's "When I am asked."

About the Author

Lubna Safi was born in Detroit and grew up in the Midwest. She is currently completing a PhD at the University of California, Berkeley. Along with poetry, Lubna writes literary criticism, fiction, and essays. *Your Blue and the Quiet Lament* is her first poetry collection.